Coming Soon:
HEAVEN

When you wake up on the other side of death, where will you be?

Terry Lee Roberts

Quotations marked **NIV** are taken from The Holy Bible: New International Version. Grand Rapids: Zondervan, 1996, 1984. Used by permission. All rights reserved.

Quotations marked **NLT** are taken from Tyndale House Publishers. (2004). Holy Bible: New Living Translation. "Text edition"--Spine. (2nd ed.) Wheaton, Ill.: Tyndale House Publishers. Used by permission. All rights reserved.

Quotations marked **NKJV** are taken from The New King James Version (1982) Nashville: Thomas Nelson. Used by permission. All rights reserved.

© Copyright 2015 by Terry Lee Roberts

All rights reserved, including the right to reproduce this book or portions thereof.

ISBN 9798668596577

Dedication

This book is dedicated to my wife of over 30 years, Rebecca. I have always been captivated by her love for me and belief in me. She is a gift from God.

I am deeply grateful for the book *Heaven* by Randy Alcorn and the sermon series *Heaven is My Home* by Paul Scanlon. They both inspired my study and the sermon series that inspired this book.

Coming Soon: Heaven

Table of Contents

Introduction 1

If I Should Die Before I Wake 3

He Had You in Mind 11

What About Hell? 19

From Here to Eternity 25

You Will Like This Place 33

The New Heaven and the New Earth 39

What is Our Purpose in Eternity? 47

What is Our Purpose Now? 53

Heaven is Eagerly Anticipating Your Arrival 57

Why Not? 61

What Others Have Said About Eternity 67

A Place for You 73

For Further Study 77

Coming Soon: Heaven

Introduction

Most people are interested in heaven. Recent movies, books and accounts of personal visits there have made us curious about what is real and what is not. Is there a heaven? What is it like? Who gets to go? Will there be animals? Can we eat food there? Those are all some of the questions to which we want answers.

Christianity Today - December, 2012

Coming Soon: Heaven

The purpose of this book is to take a fresh look at heaven and maybe even challenge some of the beliefs and ideas we have held about the afterlife. Our understanding of heaven might have been shaped by culture, movies, songs, or someone's vivid imagination. While those stories may make some good "around the campfire" conversations, they may all be untrue. In 2013, I preached a sermon series called Coming Soon: Heaven. It was well received and seemed to impart hope to Christians about their future and stimulated non- Christians to reconsider theirs. This book is the result of that series. If you don't agree with my conclusions, at least disprove them with Biblical reasons. Hopefully you will be challenged to set aside traditional thinking if you find there is no Biblical basis for it. It is helpful to think outside the box without thinking outside the Bible.

I have never visited heaven so I can't give a first-hand account. The Bible does record the story of someone who went there and came back to tell about it. He was a highly educated, credible person, held in great esteem for thousands of years by Christians in almost every denomination. That person, of course is the Apostle Paul. He records an account of going to the "third heaven" and seeing things too great for human words. His story, along with the rest of the Bible, will be the basis for our study.

If heaven is actually real and we will spend eternity there in the presence of God, it would be nice to know what is in store for us. My hope is that this book settles some questions for you and gives you a new anticipation of your eternal future.

Pastor Terry Roberts February, 2015

If I Should Die Before I Wake

Many of us were taught to pray this bedtime prayer as a child: "If I should die before I wake, I pray the Lord my soul to take." That now seems to me like a morbid and scary prayer to pray right before you close your eyes in a dark room. A typical four year old might be terrorized by the thought, even though it was intended to bring comfort. Who wants to think about death, especially right before you go to sleep?

What happens when you die? That question has been pondered by nearly every human being in every age in history. Many have speculated about the afterlife and what is "on the other side." King Solomon wrote in the Bible, *"...God has planted eternity in the hearts of men, even so, many cannot see the whole scope of God's work from beginning to end"* Ecclesiastes 3:11 NLT.

Rock singer Jackson Browne said pretty much the same thing in a song from the 1970's, "I don't know what happens when people die. Can't seem to grasp it as hard as I try. It's like a song I can hear playing right in my ear that I can't sing. I can't help listening" (From "For a Dancer" written by Jackson Browne. Copyright: Swallow Turn Music) God set eternity in the heart of man yet he can't really grasp it.

Coming Soon: Heaven

Our minds try desperately to unwrap the idea of eternity. How can something go on forever?

Science was never one of my favorite subjects in school, but I remember an elementary school science lesson about how different materials react when light is shined on them. Transparent materials allow all of the light to pass through. Opaque materials don't allow any light to pass through. The light is absorbed and turned into heat. Translucent materials allow some of the light to pass through. We cannot see through translucent materials clearly. Objects on the other side appear unclear and a little fuzzy. That is what I think Paul was referring to when he talked about our view into the eternal future. It is still a little fuzzy.

> *"For now we see through a glass, darkly; but then face to face: now I know in part; but then shall I know even as also I am known"*
> 1 Corinthians 13:12 NKJV

It seems that we all know there is more, but our human senses won't let us grasp what it is. The major religions don't share the same view of the afterlife.

The **Buddhist** believes in "Nirvana," which is a state of nothingness.

The **Hindu** has an extended vacation between reincarnations.

Purgatory was created in the minds of 3rd century philosophers to have a backup way to get sin out of the lives of those who were already dead. It didn't originate in the Bible, but was invented hundreds of years after the time of Jesus Christ by theologians. According to them, those who weren't yet good enough for heaven could undergo a purifying fire to purge the remaining evil from their hearts and lives. The idea of purgatory might owe some inspiration to Plato and other writers of his era who believed that some wicked souls could be cured by enduring temporary "therapeutic punishment" in the afterlife. The poet Dante portrayed Purgatory as a mountain which souls struggled up until they reached Paradise.

Muslim terrorists believe that if they become suicide bombers they will be ushered into bliss after death where 72 virgins await them. Paradise is defined as an eternal harem where the flesh is totally indulged.

Annihilationism teaches that human beings are totally destroyed after death and there is no hell.

Universalism teaches that all human beings spend eternity with God regardless of what they believe. Universalism doesn't believe in the doctrine of hell; only eternity with God. It is a form of "forced salvation" for everyone.

The Bible teaches against all six of those beliefs. It clearly teaches an eternity with two choices; with God, or separated from God forever. In simplest form, God gives people a choice between heaven and hell.

> *"And then he told them, "You are to go into all the world and preach the Good News to everyone, everywhere. Those who believe and are baptized will be saved. But those who refuse to believe will be condemned"*
>
> Mark 16 NLT

Jesus gave us the definition of eternal life in John 17:3 NIV: "Now this is eternal life: that they may know you, the only true God, and Jesus Christ, whom you have sent." Eternal life is living forever but it is also living on the inside. It is knowing God and being reconnected to him. Adam and Eve were separated from God when they sinned.

Eternal life is knowing God, while death is best defined as separation from God. Spiritual death is to be separated from God spiritually; physical death is to be separated from your physical body even though your spirit and soul continue to be alive and conscious, and eternal death is to enter into eternity after you physically die, not knowing God and separated from him forever. The Bible calls that "the second death."

> *"Blessed and holy are those who have part in the first resurrection. The second death has no power over them, but they will be priests of God and of Christ and will reign with him for a thousand years"*
> Revelation 20:6 NIV

> *"He will punish those who do not know God and do not obey the gospel of our Lord Jesus. They will be punished with everlasting destruction and shut out from the presence of the Lord and from the majesty of his power"*
> 2 Thessalonians 1:8-9 NIV

This elementary principal reinforces how important the message of salvation and eternal life are. Everyone lives somewhere forever. The Bible doesn't teach the idea that we cease to exist after we die (annihilationism), or that we come back again as something or someone else (reincarnation). Jesus gave us the hope of eternity at the resurrection of Lazarus when he said; *"...I am the resurrection and the life. He who believes in me will live, even though he dies; and whoever lives and believes in me will never die. Do you believe this?"* John 11:25-26 NIV

We get to live forever even when we physically die because physical death is not the end. It is very important to settle the issue of where you go after you die before you physically die. After you die physically, it is too late to choose. Choose Jesus and eternal life. Eternity with him is much better than eternity without him.

It is possible to live your life as a follower of Jesus Christ and not fear death. Where you will spend eternity is the nagging question we all carry around in the back of our minds. Once that question is answered and your eternity is settled you can live in peace. You are not really ready to live until you are ready to die.

> *"Because God's children are human beings—made of flesh and blood—the Son also became flesh and blood. For only as a human being could he die, and only by dying could he break the power of the devil, who had the power of death. Only in this way could he set free all who have lived their lives as slaves to the fear of dying"*
> Hebrews 2:14-15 NLT

Some people have died tormented by fear. Others have died fearlessly knowing their next breath would be on the other side of this life with Jesus in a better place. Paul the apostle said it was better by far to die and be with Christ. He said to be absent from the body is to be present with the Lord and that to die was gain. When someone dies we say we "lost" them. Heaven gains them. On the earth we say "they are going." In eternity they say "here they come!"

Someone made a list of some of the famous last words of people before they died. These are the last words of some famous people:

LADY NANCY ASTOR *"Am I dying or is this my birthday?"*

THOMAS CRANMER, Archbishop of Canterbury *"I see Heaven open and Jesus on the right hand of God."*

Coming Soon: Heaven

JOHN WESLEY-"Best of all, Jesus is with us."

SIR ARTHUR CONAN DOYLE - He wrote the Sherlock Holmes stories and died at age 71 in his garden. He turned to his wife and said, *"You are wonderful,"* then clutched his chest and died.

T.S. ELIOT - The writer was only able to whisper one word as he died: *"Valerie,"* the name of his wife.

STEPHEN, THE FIRST MARTYR *"Look, I see the heavens opened and the Son of Man standing in the place of honor at God's right hand!"* Acts 6:56 NLT

Some less famous people:

"Nice Doggie."

"I wonder where the mother bear is."

"Anyone know what this wire is for?"

"Hey guys, Watch this!"

A great story is told about a Christian man driving home with a son who was highly allergic to bee stings. A bee was tormenting the boy and the father couldn't get it to fly out of the car window so he grabbed the bee with his hand, squeezed it and let it fly again. The boy asked his dad why he had let the bee go and the father opened his hand to reveal the stinger. The bee may still be in the car with you, but its stinger is gone. Death lost its sting when it stung Jesus.

If I Should Die Before I Wake

"Where, O death, is your victory? Where, O death, is your sting?"
1 Corinthians 15:55 NIV

Settle your eternal destiny by trusting Jesus to forgive and save you and you can live the rest of your life free from the fear of death. Jesus tasted death so we don't have to fear it ever again. Death has been cured by Jesus Christ. He conquered death, and the sting of death has been removed.

He Had You in Mind

"Let not your heart be troubled; you believe in God, believe also in Me. In My Father's house are many mansions; if it were not so, I would have told you. I go to prepare a place for you. And if I go and prepare a place for you, I will come again and receive you to Myself; that where I am, there you may be also."

John 14:1-3 NKJV

When Jesus Christ made the above statement, he was facing the cross. He was looking beyond the coming emotional and spiritual pain to a future after his resurrection and after your resurrection. He went to the cross despising the shame, but looking forward to the joy set before him. That joy was a picture of you and me with him in eternity, enjoying the fruit and results of his death, burial and resurrection. He had come from heaven and was going back. He didn't want to go home alone.

It has been said that Jesus' statement here is the *greatest promise* ever made, about the *greatest place* ever imagined, by the *greatest person* who ever lived. He was giving his reason for persevering through trials and trouble. That is our reason as well. For the joy set before us, we endure. In order to endure we need a better picture of the joy. The joy of Jesus was that what he was doing would make it possible for those who trusted him to follow him home to the Father to a place we loosely call heaven. On the other side of this earth lies a place that the Bible refers to as "Paradise." What did Jesus reveal to us from this promise about eternity?

Heaven is a Place

Many theologians have strayed from what the Bible actually says about heaven and suggest that nothing in our present reality tells us anything about what our future will be like. The truth is, our present earth gives us many clues about what the new earth will be like. For instance: it has gates, it has a city in it, it is marked by many of the same things present on planet earth, and it is literally a place.

When God speaks about the future, he uses terms like city and country. If it were not city and country like we understand and identify with here on this earth, he would have said so. We can spend eternity in a place like this place, only flawless!

There is no reason to believe heaven will be absent of streets, trees, animals, rivers, and maybe Harley Davidsons. We will enjoy it there as we eat and laugh. It will be filled with bright colors and music. God is creative. Why would he create a beige, boring eternity for himself or us? It just doesn't fit his nature.

It has been said that maybe the reason heaven comes across as austere and cold is that the descriptions of eternity and books written about it in the past have usually been written by men in a cold library somewhere, much like my apartment when I was a single man. Maybe there should be descriptions of eternity written by women, to give it life and color. We have often seen the skeleton of eternity minus the body and essence of it.

Time and space are part of earth but since there will be a New Earth, why do we believe time, space, and physical laws will pass away? There will be a New Heaven and a New Earth, according to the Bible. It appears that followers of Jesus will have access to both. Earth itself will remain a physical place after the order of the Garden of Eden, before sin and the curse of death came to the earth. Because of that, it will have a striking similarity to the earth we now live on. Time and space will still exist, but man will not be limited by it.

My way of understanding the new earth compared to this present one comes from a movie you probably watched growing up called *The Wizard of Oz*. Before Dorothy and her dog Toto landed in Oz, they were in Kansas where everything was black and white. When they landed in Oz, thanks to the recent discovery of color technology in Hollywood, everything was in color. We are living in a black and white Kansas, waiting for Oz in living color!

> *"...No eye has seen, no ear has heard, and no mind has imagined what God has prepared for those who love him"*
>
> 1 Corinthians 2:9 NLT

You Will Have a Body

When most people think about heaven and eternity they seem to think people will no longer have a physical body, but simply be a spirit. In the beginning God formed man's body out of the dust before he breathed life into him. Man was a physical body first (Genesis 2:7). Jesus demonstrated the prototype for our new physical bodies after he was resurrected from the dead. He ate, walked through a wall, and took a walk with his friends on the Emmaus Road. He later revealed himself to his other disciples.

Coming Soon: Heaven

"While they were still talking about this, Jesus himself stood among them and said to them, "Peace be with you." They were startled and frightened, thinking they saw a ghost. He said to them, "Why are you troubled, and why do doubts rise in your minds? Look at my hands and my feet. It is I myself! Touch me and see; a ghost does not have flesh and bones, as you see I have"
Luke 24:36-39 NIV

In eternity our bodies will be physical, yet not subject to disease or death. Our present bodies are growing old and are subject to the fallen world. They are actually a part of the fallen creation, but our new bodies will not have a connection to sin and death.

Someone said that the most beautiful person ever seen on earth is still a product of the curse. There is a down payment of physical death lurking even in the most spry and attractive among us. What a great joy it will be to live in a body that is not subject to sickness, death or pain. Just imagine a physical body that doesn't age or ever get gray hair. Think of the money we will all save on make-up and cosmetics!

Yet what we suffer now is nothing compared to the glory he will reveal to us later. For all creation is waiting eagerly for that future day when God will reveal who his children really are. Against its will, all creation was subjected to God's curse. But with eager hope, the creation looks forward to the day when it will join God's children in glorious freedom from death and decay. For we know that all creation has been groaning as in the pains of childbirth right up to the present time. And we believers also groan, even though we have the Holy Spirit within us as a foretaste of future glory, for we long for our bodies to be released from sin and suffering. We, too, wait with eager hope for the day when God will give us our full

He Had You In Mind

rights as his adopted children, including the new bodies he has promised us"
Romans 8:18-23 NLT

t is interesting in the Apostle Paul's story of going to the third heaven that he didn't know if he was in the body or out of the body. He said that only God knew, and the implication was that it seemed the same to him. He wasn't even aware of any change. We should focus less on the differences between our bodies now and our new body, and more on the similarities of our eternity to now. We will get a body that is an upgraded model but much like the one we now have.

"Dear friends, we are already God's children, but he has not yet shown us what we will be like when Christ appears. But we do know that we will be like him, for we will see him as he really is."
1 John 3:2 NLT

Jesus' followers will live forever as spiritual and physical people. Our future bodies will certainly bear the resemblance of our present bodies, as illustrated in the story of the rich man and Lazarus in Luke 16. The rich man recognized Lazarus, and even remembered back to his time on earth.

You Will Know Even as You are Known

Many have held to the notion that when someone goes into eternity, their memory banks will be erased. As we see in the case of Lazarus and the rich man, that isn't the case. What if I went up to my wife, Becky in eternity and said, "There is just something about you! Do I know you from somewhere?" That would be ridiculous. Even though we will no longer be married, I will not cease to know her or remember that we were married. There is a sense that God protects you from what is harmful to your memories because in heaven he will *"wipe every tear from our eyes and there will be no more crying or death."*

The Bible says we will actually know as we are known which implies that our understanding will greatly increase. That is as simple as removing the effects of sin and death from our brains and souls.

"Now we see things imperfectly, like puzzling reflections in a mirror, but then we will see everything with perfect clarity. All that I know now is partial and incomplete, but then I will know everything completely, just as God now knows me completely"
1 Corinthians 13:12 NLT

We will have wonderful transparent relationships in eternity. They will not be robotic interactions with strangers. They will be part of our family. Paul says that there is family in heaven and family on earth. In the Old Testament when a patriarch died they would say they were *gathered to their family*. That is a hope filled way to understand death and passing from this life into the next.

"For this reason I bow my knees to the Father of our Lord Jesus Christ, from whom the whole family in heaven and earth is named"
Ephesians 3:14-15 NKJV

You Will Have Direct Physical Access to God

The Bible teaches that in eternity God himself will live among men. That is an amazing thought. Jesus himself said in the

He Had You In Mind

Sermon on the Mount, *"Blessed are the pure in heart, <u>for they will see God</u>"* Matthew 5:8 NIV

That was the joy that was set before Jesus: the picture of you and me as followers of Jesus, experiencing the Father as he had. He had hope of spending eternity with us in his Father's house. He said he was going there to get it ready for us. That kept Jesus on the cross; the joy of your eternity with him. He had you and me in mind when he was giving his life. He made it very clear before he left that he wants us there with him. The cross and his impending death were on his mind when he spoke about coming to get you and me and take us to where he will be. He was able to face separation from the Father and death because he had us in his mind.

What About Hell?

In 2003, a study found that 64% of Americans thought they would go to heaven when they died, but less than 1% thought they would go to hell. Jesus spent more time on the subject of hell than any other Biblical author. Why was it necessary? As a matter of fact, why is hell itself necessary?

The purpose of this book is to study and explore the wonders of the coming ages in the presence of God. In order to make an honest assessment of eternity with God, it is necessary to look at the alternative. That alternative is hell, separated from God and left to ourselves for eternity. To think of a loved one or friend going there is enough to almost cause physical anguish.

In the previous chapter, we defined death as separation. The separation of our spirits from our bodies is physical death; our spirits from God is spiritual death, and eternal separation from God is the *second death* as the Bible calls it.

> *"He will punish those who do not know God and do not obey the gospel of our Lord Jesus. They will be punished with everlasting destruction and shut out from the presence of the Lord and from the glory of his might"*
>
> 2 Thessalonians 1:8-9 NIV

Coming Soon: Heaven

We have all probably heard people jokingly remark about partying with their friends in hell as if it were a music festival or never-ending party. Jesus spent so much time telling the truth about hell, because he presents it as something far less than a good experience where rebels against God get to go and revel in their independent attitude for eternity. Hell is void of relationships. A relationship with God or other people is impossible. Man's ability to relate and connect with others is from God. It is his creation and idea. Apart from him, relationships won't exist.

God is life, love, and light itself. To be separated from him and the very things that make this life enjoyable is beyond comprehension. Jesus himself warned against hell in Matthew 25:

> *"Then he will say to those on his left, 'Depart from me, you who are cursed, into the eternal fire prepared for the devil and his angels...' Then they will go away to eternal punishment, but the righteous to eternal life"*
>
> Matthew 25:41,46 NIV

One of the words Jesus used for hell was *Gehenna*. It was a garbage dump that burned continually outside the city of Jerusalem. In Mark 9:43- 44, he refers to Gehenna as the place where the fire is not quenched and the worm does not die. Jesus was referring to the maggots that lived in the corpses on the garbage dump. Those corpses without families to bury them would be thrown on this never dying fire. In another place, Jesus refers to hell as *outer darkness*.

Hell is therefore, according to the Scriptures above, defined as a place of separation, isolation, decomposition, and disintegration. It is a place of misery and hopelessness due to the eternal state of those who go there. The most severe condemnation Jesus ever gave was *"depart from me."* That is the worst thing that could ever happen to us because we were designed by God to receive our life from him and his presence. To be outside of the presence of God, is to leave a person as an empty shell. Even those who reject God and rebel against him receive their life from him in this present life.

Hell was created for the devil and his followers. God never desired for men to go there. The cost of having a family that chose to spend eternity with you is offering those who didn't want to be with you a legitimate alternative. Unfortunately, hell is that alternative. God made man in his image to be eternal. Every person will go somewhere forever, according to the Bible. A person does not cease to exist when they die physically.

What is hell, then? It is God actively giving us up to what we have freely chosen - to go our own way, to be …*"the master of our fate, the captain of our soul,"* to get away from him and his control. It is God banishing us to regions we have desperately tried to get into all our lives.

"Scripture sees hell as self-chosen - [H]ell appears as God's gesture of respect for human choice. All receive what they actually chose, either to be with God forever, worshipping him, or without God forever, worshipping themselves" (J.I. Packer, *Concise Theology* p.262-263).

"If the thing you most want is to worship God in the beauty of his holiness, then that is what you will get (Ps 96:9-13). If the thing you most want is to be your own master, then the holiness of God will become an agony, and the presence of God a terror you will flee forever (Rev 6:16; cf. Is 6:1-6)" ("The Importance of Hell" from Timothy Keller in *The Redeemer Report*, August, 2009).

"There are only two kinds of people in the end: those who say to God, 'Thy will be done,' and those to whom God says, in the end, 'Thy will be done.' All that are in Hell, choose it. Without that self-choice there could be no Hell. No soul that seriously and

Coming Soon: Heaven

constantly desires joy will ever miss it. Those who seek find. Those who knock it is opened" (C.S. Lewis in The Great Divorce)

Paul Scanlon said the only thing a person has to do to go to hell is nothing. Hell is the default mode for the human race. Jesus came to remove the sentence of condemnation that rested on all of humanity.

> *"For God did not send his Son into the world to condemn the world, but to save the world through him. Whoever believes in him is not condemned, but whoever does not believe stands condemned already because they have not believed in the name of God's one and only Son"*
>
> John 3:17-18 *NIV*

Jesus was so much against people going to hell that he gave his life and went into the heart of the earth himself, so that all people would have the opportunity to skip hell.

The Bible tells a story about two men who died. One went to Hades (Hell) and the other went to Abraham's side (Paradise). There is too much detail for this to be a parable. It records names and specifics that lead us to believe Jesus was telling about actual events.

> *"There was a rich man who was dressed in purple and fine linen and lived in luxury every day. At his gate was laid a beggar named Lazarus, covered with sores and longing to eat what fell from the rich man's table. Even the dogs came and licked his sores.*
>
> *"The time came when the beggar died and the angels carried him to Abraham's side. The rich man also died and was buried. In Hades, where he was in torment, he looked up and saw Abraham far away, with Lazarus by his side. So he called to him, 'Father Abraham, have pity on me and send Lazarus to dip the tip of his finger in water and cool my tongue, because I am in agony in this fire.'*

What About Hell?

"But Abraham replied, 'Son, remember that in your lifetime you received your good things, while Lazarus received bad things, but now he is comforted here and you are in agony. And besides all this, between us and you a great chasm has been set in place, so that those who want to go from here to you cannot, nor can anyone cross over from there to us.'
"He answered, 'Then I beg you, father, send Lazarus to my family, for I have five brothers. Let him warn them, so that they will not also come to this place of torment.'
"Abraham replied, 'They have Moses and the Prophets; let them listen to them.'
"'No, father Abraham,' he said, 'but if someone from the dead goes to them, they will repent.'
"He said to him, 'If they do not listen to Moses and the Prophets, they will not be convinced even if someone rises from the dead'"

Luke 16:19-31 NIV

Notice that the man who was in Hades had memories and regrets. He didn't lose consciousness after he died. He remembered his life, his mistakes, and his obvious bad decision not to follow God into eternity. He had total recall. Some theologians have taught the idea of *soul sleep*. That is a state of unconsciousness in the in-between of death and eternity. Nothing in Scripture supports that idea.

Hell isn't so much about physical suffering as much as it is being left to experience the screaming loneliness and hopelessness of going into eternity separated from God and separated from true life.

Dr. J.P. Moreland, an American philosopher, theologian, and Christian apologist made the following statements about hell:

"Actually, hell was not part of the original creation. Hell is God's fallback position. Hell is something God was forced to make

because people chose to rebel against Him and turn against what was best for them and the purpose for which they were created."

"...He has made us with free-will and He has made us for a purpose: to relate lovingly to Him and to others… if we fail over and over again to live for the purpose for which we were made, then God will have absolutely no choice but to give us what we've asked for all along in our lives, which is separation from Him. And that is hell…"

"It's wrong to think that God is simply a loving being… yes God is a compassionate being, but He's also a just, moral and pure being. So God's decisions are not based on modern American sentimentalism… they've forgotten the hard virtues of holiness, righteousness and justice."

G.K. Chesterton said, *"Hell is God's great compliment to the reality of human freedom and the dignity of human choice."* In other words, God hates hell but because he made humans eternal, he left himself no choice but to allow those who demand their freedom and independence a place to be separated from him eternally.

God is still speaking the same words to humanity that he spoke through Joshua in the Old Testament:

> *"Today I have given you the choice between life and death, between blessings and curses. Now I call on heaven and earth to witness the choice you make. Oh, that you would choose life, so that you and your descendants might live!"*
>
> Deuteronomy 30:19 NLT

From Here to Eternity

End time events are controversial and often fodder for arguments among Bible believing followers of Jesus. We may disagree with the exact journey from where we are now in history to eternity breaking through, but hopefully our end result is the same. If you disagree with the sequence of events laid out here, remember we have eternity to straighten each other out! Hold on, you are going to like what happens next.

As I write this book, there is a new buzz about Jesus returning soon because of the blood moons coming this year and the alliance of the nations as prophesied in the Old Testament. The Prime Minister of Israel has just issued a call to Jews everywhere to return to Israel to avoid the coming persecution. Those, along with many other current events make you wonder if Jesus will come back before this book is even finished. He could. On the other hand, he could come back in one hundred years. As my German friend said, "Even if this is not the last generation; it is my last generation!" We should live as though Jesus will not return in our lifetime, but be ready to meet him today if he comes.

The real question that is being asked is, "What happens next?" What can we look forward to as Christians, or dread if we are not? Your understanding of the end time events will affect your decisions and choices. John said, anyone who has the hope of Jesus' return *purifies himself*. If Jesus is coming soon, it is a great motivation to live right.

The next event for you may be physical death. If you die as a follower of Jesus Christ, you go immediately into the presence of the Lord. To be absent from the body is to be present with the Lord. A Christian who dies is conscious and aware of where they are. Even though a believer is conscious in their soul and mind, they will not receive a new body until Jesus returns to the earth. Christians who die before Jesus returns go to Paradise, which is sometimes referred to as an *intermediary heaven*. That is not a Biblical term but the idea is that you are conscious and in the presence of the Lord but haven't yet received a physical body. Christians who die before the consummation of the end of the age remain in this place, also known as Paradise awaiting the physical resurrection. The term *intermediary heaven* is used to distinguish it from the *eternal heaven* at the end of the age. Paul addressed this subject in his letter to the Thessalonian church. They were asking questions about Christians who had already died. What was their fate?

> *"And now, dear brothers and sisters, we want you to know what will happen to the believers who have died so you will not grieve like people who have no hope. For since we believe that Jesus died and was raised to life again, we also believe that when Jesus returns, God will bring back with him the believers who have died.*
>
> *We tell you this directly from the Lord: We who are still living when the Lord returns will not meet him ahead of those who have died. For the Lord himself will come down from heaven with a commanding shout, with the voice of the archangel, and with the trumpet call of God. First, the believers who have died will rise from their graves. Then, together with them, we who are still alive and remain on the earth will be caught up in the clouds to meet the Lord*

From Here To Eternity

in the air. Then we will be with the Lord forever. So encourage each other with these words"

1 Thessalonians 4:13-18NLT

Paul was taken to the *third heaven* to the very presence of God and he said he wasn't aware if he was there physically with his body or not. It obviously seemed the same to him as it did when he was on the earth. He wasn't aware of his body. Believers who have died will be in much the same state as they await a new body. In the Old Testament, those who were trusting God for salvation and waiting for the Messiah were taken to a place called *Abraham's Bosom*, also known as *Paradise*. When Jesus died and rose from the dead, he moved Paradise from the heart of the earth to the presence of God. He told the thief on the cross that he would be with him that day in Paradise.

Unbelievers who die suffer a much worse fate. They are conscious as well, but they are taken to a place in the heart of the earth known as *hell* or *hades*. In the Old Testament, it was called *Sheol* or *Abaddon*. It is the place of the dead. These people are conscious in their soul and mind as well. (Refer to the story of the rich man and Lazarus who died.)

These unbelievers are awaiting the final judgment which is described in Revelation 20:11-15:

> *"And I saw a great white throne and the one sitting on it. The earth and sky fled from his presence, but they found no place to hide. I saw the dead, both great and small, standing before God's throne. And the books were opened, including the Book of Life. And the dead were judged according to what they had done, as recorded in the books. The sea gave up its dead, and death and the grave gave up their dead. And all were judged according to their deeds. Then death and the grave were thrown into the lake of fire. This lake of fire is the second death. And anyone whose name was not found recorded in the Book of Life was thrown into the lake of fire"*

Coming Soon: Heaven

This event doesn't occur for at least 1000 years (after the millennial reign of Jesus Christ physically over the earth), so the dead remain in that state for quite some time.

Those who remain alive until Jesus Christ returns, will experience a catching away to meet the Lord in the air.

> "...First, the believers who have died will rise from their graves. Then, together with them, we who are still alive and remain on the earth will be caught up in the clouds to meet the Lord in the air. Then we will be with the Lord forever. So encourage each other with these words"
>
> 1 Thessalonians 4:16-18 NLT

The term *caught up* in the original language is *harpázō*. The meaning of this word is *to seize upon, spoil, and snatch away*. This catching away is known as the *rapture*. There is much discussion among Christians about when this event happens. Some believe it is before the earth is judged and some believe it is after. Either way, according to Paul, it will happen to one generation in history. Maybe we are that generation!

After Jesus catches away his church, all believers will go before *the judgment seat of Christ*. This is a time when rewards will be given for the stewardship of their gifts and calling.

> *"For we must all stand before Christ to be judged. We will each receive whatever we deserve for the good or evil we have done in this earthly body"*
>
> 2 Corinthians 5:10 NLT

This isn't a judgment to determine whether or not the person is a Christian. This is a judgment of the Christian in order to provide an award or reward for their life as a Christian. All believers will have to "pass through the fire" to see what is burned up and what remains.

> *"Anyone who builds on that foundation may use a variety of materials—gold, silver, jewels, wood, hay, or straw. But on the judgment day, fire will reveal what kind of work each builder has done. The fire will show if a person's work has any value. If the work survives, that builder will receive a reward. But if the work is burned up, the builder will suffer great loss. The builder will be saved, but like someone barely escaping through a wall of flames"*
> 1 Corinthians 3:12-15 NLT

Christians are saved by grace through faith. We have been given new life and a responsibility to share this new life with others. After Jesus returns, Christians will have to give an account for how they used this gift and trust to help others. (See 2 Corinthians 5:10, Hebrews 9:28, and 1 Corinthians 3:11-15)

What was done in this life in obedience to the Holy Spirit and the Word of God will determine a lot about the quality of the Christian's eternity. Some will be saved but lose their rewards. The Bible lists several *crowns* or rewards to be given out based on the motive of the heart. It isn't just a matter of *what* you did but *why* you did it.

- The crown of life - James 1:12
- An imperishable crown - 1 Corinthians 9:24-27
- The crown of exultation - 1 Thessalonians 2:19-20
- The crown of righteousness - 2 Timothy 4:5-8
- The crown of glory - 1 Peter 5:2-4

These are probably not the only rewards to be given out. Exactly what they are isn't revealed. The conclusion is that we will give an account for the time, talent, and treasure entrusted to us, (For a more in-depth look at judgments see my book, *The Healthy Christian Life*)

Those present at the judgment seat of Christ are to be *rewarded and reassigned.* Eternity is just beginning, and your role in the coming ages begins now!

After this awards-ceremony is an event known as *The Marriage Supper of the Lamb.* This seems to be a big party, like a wedding reception. Present will be Abraham, Moses, Paul, Mary, Peter and hopefully you and me. This is the fulfillment and completion of the Passover supper Jesus had with his disciples before he was crucified. What a party! Jesus said everyone who is invited to this party is blessed.

The Bible then records what the Israelites were looking for all along; the physical rule of the Messiah over planet earth. Every *-ism* will become a *-wasm* when Jesus Christ, the Prince of Peace takes his throne to rule with righteousness and justice over planet earth. This event is spoken of in the Old Testament and New Testament. Revelation 20 (NLT) gives an account of the events that happen in their correct order:

Satan is Bound (Revelation 20:1-6)

"Then I saw an angel coming down from heaven with the key to the bottomless pit and a heavy chain in his hand. He seized the dragon—that old serpent, who is the devil, Satan—and bound him in chains for a thousand years. The angel threw him into the bottomless pit, which he then shut and locked so Satan could not deceive the nations anymore until the thousand years were finished. Afterward he must be released for a little while.

Then I saw thrones, and the people sitting on them had been given the authority to judge. And I saw the souls of those who had been beheaded for their testimony about Jesus and for proclaiming the word of God. They had not worshiped the beast or his statue, nor accepted his mark on their foreheads or their hands. They all came to life again, and they reigned with Christ for a thousand years.

This is the first resurrection. (The rest of the dead did not come back to life until the thousand years had ended.) Blessed and holy are those who share in the first resurrection. For them the second death holds no power, but they will be priests of God and of Christ and will reign with him a thousand years."

The Defeat of Satan (Revelation 20:7-10)

"When the thousand years come to an end, Satan will be let out of his prison. He will go out to deceive the nations—called Gog and Magog—in every corner of the earth. He will gather them together for battle—a mighty army, as numberless as sand along the seashore. And I saw them as they went up on the broad plain of the earth and surrounded God's people and the beloved city. But fire from heaven came down on the attacking armies and consumed them. Then the devil, who had deceived them, was thrown into the fiery lake of burning sulfur, joining the beast and the false prophet. There they will be tormented day and night forever and ever."

The Final Judgment of unbelievers (Revelation 20:11-15)

"And I saw a great white throne and the one sitting on it. The earth and sky fled from his presence, but they found no place to hide. I saw the dead, both great and small, standing before God's throne. And the books were opened, including the Book of Life. And the dead were judged according to what they had done, as recorded in the books. The sea gave up its dead, and death and the grave gave up their dead. And all were judged according to their deeds. Then death and the grave were thrown into the lake of fire. This lake of fire is the second death. And anyone whose name was not found recorded in the Book of Life was thrown into the lake of fire"

Coming Soon: Heaven

Now that evil is dealt with and rewards have been handed out to the faithful, it is time to get on with eternity. Up until this time, all of the events have occurred on this present earth. Jesus literally reigns over the present planet earth for one thousand years. Now it is time for a New Heaven and a New Earth. Revelation 21 records this new creation.

> *"Then I saw a new heaven and a new earth, for the old heaven and the old earth had disappeared. And the sea was also gone. And I saw the holy city, the New Jerusalem, coming down from God out of heaven like a bride beautifully dressed for her husband.*
>
> *I heard a loud shout from the throne, saying, 'Look, God's home is now among his people! He will live with them, and they will be his people. God himself will be with them He will wipe every tear from their eyes, and there will be no more death or sorrow or crying or pain. All these things are gone forever.'*
>
> *And the one sitting on the throne said, 'Look, I am making everything new!' And then he said to me, 'Write this down, for what I tell you is trustworthy and true.' And he also said, 'It is finished! I am the Alpha and the Omega—the Beginning and the End. To all who are thirsty I will give freely from the springs of the water of life. All who are victorious will inherit all these blessings, and I will be their God, and they will be my children'"*
>
> Revelation 21:1-7 NLT

This is where we will live forever with God in a place with no death or crying. God himself will live among the human race and finally justice and mercy will reign in the universe. The earth will be a paradise, much like Eden with no curse. The old order of things has passed away and all things have become new.

You Will Like This Place

Heaven has not had an appeal to many people simply because it seemed so "other worldly." As a child I somehow picked up the idea that heaven would be everyone in a big room in choir robes singing songs. What a bore! Who wants to spend eternity in a never-ending church service?

God is a creator. He is creative. The idea that we will just hang out for eternity doesn't fit with who he is or with who he has made us to be. Work and activity are part of our future. We will *rule and reign* with him. Jesus tells a parable about an eternal reward for being faithful, being assigned the care of cities. (Luke 19:12-26) Exactly what we will be doing isn't clear from Scripture, but it certainly will not be a place of no activity or creativity. That would not reflect who God is and who we are. It isn't wise to over speculate where Scripture is silent. We are told the nature of our future, but not the specifics of it.

> *"Let not your heart be troubled; you believe in God, believe also in Me. In My Father's house are many mansions; if it were not so, I would have told you. I go to prepare a place for you. And if I go*

Coming Soon: Heaven

and prepare a place for you, I will come again and receive you to Myself; that where I am, there you may be also"
John 14:1-3 NKJ

Jesus made it very clear that he was going to prepare a *place* for us. We know what a place is. (The dictionary defines it as a space, area, or spot, set apart or used for a particular purpose.) That is relevant to us because we often think of heaven as just being a part of space or a gathering of clouds.

When a couple is expecting a child, they often begin preparing a room for him. It is decorated and painted to match the gender. Great effort is taken to make sure everything will be ready before the baby arrives. That is the idea Jesus is getting across. He went ahead of us to get a place ready *for us*. It isn't a generic place, but a very specific, custom made place that Jesus is personally overseeing to make sure it fits your specifications. Heaven will not be surprised by your arrival. For at least 2000 years, God has been getting a place ready for you, and the Holy Spirit is working in us to get us ready for the place.

Earth is in many ways a mirror of heaven. Even though the earth is flawed, much of what we see on earth had its origin in heaven. In heaven, there will be rivers, food, animals, trees and so many of the other things that we love on earth. We will have a physical body that is free from the curse of death. Jesus was raised from the dead physically and we are to receive a body like his. We will have a physical body for eternity. We will be able to run, walk, eat, and touch with it.

Heaven will be a wonderful place. In his book The Weight of Glory, C.S. Lewis notes how believers often underestimate the full riches God has for His children.

"...If we consider...the staggering nature of the rewards promised in the Gospels, it would seem that our Lord finds our desires, not too

You Will Like This Place

strong, but too weak. We are half-hearted creatures...like an ignorant child who wants to go on making mud pies in a slum because he cannot imagine what is meant by the offer of a holiday at the sea. We are far too easily pleased."

To understand God's future plan for mankind, it is helpful to look back at Eden. God created magnificent surroundings for men and women in the garden. The weather was great, the vegetation was stunning, the animals were harmless, and it was a great place to live. In the same way that God created a land filled with life and bright colors and great smells, why wouldn't that be part of our future? Notice also that Adam and Eve were to have a job in the garden. They weren't created to sit around all day. Part of God's nature is to expand his creation and rule. That will be part of our eternity with him as well.

In Randy Alcorn's book *Heaven*, he discusses the false idea that heaven is completely different from the earth.

"When Jesus told his disciples, 'In my Father's house are many rooms...I am going there to prepare a place for you' (John 14:2), he deliberately chose common, physical terms (house, rooms, place), to describe where he was going and what he was preparing for us. He wanted to give his disciples (and us) something tangible to look forward to - an actual place where they (and we) would go to be with him."

The apostle Paul spoke to the Romans about the strong inner desire that we have to finally arrive at that place where we are most at home. Even the creation itself is straining towards that end.

"Yet what we suffer now is nothing compared to the glory he will reveal to us later. For all creation is waiting eagerly for that future

Coming Soon: Heaven

day when God will reveal who his children really are. Against its will, all creation was subjected to God's curse. But with eager hope, the creation looks forward to the day when it will join God's children in glorious freedom from death and decay. For we know that all creation has been groaning as in the pains of childbirth right up to the present time. And we believers also groan, even though we have the Holy Spirit within us as a foretaste of future glory, for we long for our bodies to be released from sin and suffering. We, too, wait with eager hope for the day when God will give us our full rights as his adopted children, including the new bodies he has promised us. We were given this hope when we were saved. (If we already have something, we don't need to hope for it. But if we look forward to something we don't yet have, we must wait patiently and confidently)"

Romans 8:18-25 NLT

We innately know that this present life is not the ultimate existence. We are not completely at home here.

C.S. Lewis said it as well as anyone ever has,

"If I find in myself a desire which no experience in this world can satisfy, the most probable explanation is that I was made for another world" (Mere Christianity New York: Collier Books, 1960, 120).

That sums up our inability to be completely at home; we were made for another world!

He expanded that thought in *The Problem of Pain* (New York: Macmillan, 1962, 115):

"The settled happiness and security which we all desire, God withholds from us by the very nature of the world: but joy, pleasure, and merriment He has scattered broadcast. We are never safe, but

You Will Like This Place

we have plenty of fun, and some ecstasy. It is not hard to see why. The security we crave would teach us to rest our hearts in this world and oppose an obstacle to our return to God."

As we saw in the example of the rich man and Lazarus, those who died were still recognizable and had their own identity. You and I will not disappear into the robotic sameness as everyone else. We are God's unique creation for all of eternity. You will still be you in eternity. Your heart is drawn to a place that is more like your real home than where you are now.

We can look forward to enjoying things there in fullness that we enjoyed here in part. That may be riding horses, sports, driving vehicles, or who knows what? I would ask *"Why not?"*

Our relationship with God will take on a new dimension but also our relationships with others. Paul said that we would know and love more fully in eternity.

"For now we see only a reflection as in a mirror; then we shall see face to face. Now I know in part; then I shall know fully, even as I am fully known. And now these three remain: faith, hope and love. But the greatest of these is love"
1 Corinthians 13 NIV

God is love and the atmosphere around him is love. What a great place to be!

"I have come home at last! This is my real country! I belong here. This is the land I have been looking for all my life, though I never knew it till now...Come further up, come further in!" (C.S. Lewis in The Last Battle)

We are all invited to eternity with God because of the sacrifice of Jesus Christ for our sins. It is important to understand that the default mode for human beings is hell. Just like you

Coming Soon: Heaven

respond to an invitation to a party or wedding reception, if you plan on going to heaven, you must send in your RSVP (French: répondez s'il vous plait which means *please respond*.) You are invited. Jesus has a place prepared for you. Have you sent in your RSVP yet?

The New Heaven and the New Earth

Christians often say, *I am going to heaven after I die.* It would be just as Biblically accurate to say *I am going to live on the New Earth.* It is even better to just say, *I am going into eternity with God.* The point is that we will live forever as physical beings on a physical earth. We will have access to the New Heaven but it seems our lives will be lived primarily on the New Earth in the New Jerusalem. Someone said the New Heaven will be on the New Earth. Wherever it is, you get both!

If you have traveled, it is likely that you have seen some breathtaking scenery and sights. You may have seen the Grand Canyon, the Swiss Alps, Donegal, Ireland on a misty day, or any number of stunning displays of God's creation. As breathtaking as some scenery can be, we have only seen the "black and white" version of our planet. As wonderful as it is, this planet is only a shadow of what God intended it to be.

Paul Scanlon in his series on heaven jokingly said,

> *"Heaven is where the cooks are French, the comedians are English, the mechanics are German, the lovers are Italian, and everything is organized by the Swiss. Hell on the other hand is where the cooks*

Coming Soon: Heaven

are English, the comedians are German, the mechanics are French, the lovers are Swiss, and everything is organized by the Italians."

The point is that eternity is where what is upside-down will be turned right-side up.

The curse of sin, death, and decay has marred earth almost beyond recognition compared to what it was before. Paradise lost in Eden will someday be Paradise found on the New Earth. It will be better than Eden. The colors, smells, sounds, and sights will be enough to take your breath away.

What marks and identifies this New Earth? Why will it be so different from the earth we live on now? Much of what marks the New Earth is what is absent. God chose a great term to describe what would be absent, *no more*.

> No more death.
> No more crying.
> No more pain.
> No more curse.

Someone said, *Eternity swallows up in a moment the sorrows of a lifetime*. The overwhelming sense in eternity will be the absence of enemies. The world, the flesh, and the devil will have been dealt with. Temptation is gone. Righteousness, peace, and joy reign in every thought and every action. It will be marked by a tangible peace that passes mere understanding.

In the Old Testament, God spoke to the prophet Isaiah about the New Earth he would create.

"Look! I am creating new heavens and a new earth, and no one will even think about the old ones anymore. Be glad; rejoice forever in my creation! And look! I will create Jerusalem as a place of happiness. Her people will be a source of joy. I will rejoice over Jerusalem and

The New Heaven and The New Earth

delight in my people. And the sound of weeping and crying will be heard in it no more. No longer will babies die when only a few days old. No longer will adults die before they have lived a full life. No longer will people be considered old at one hundred! Only the cursed will die that young! In those days people will live in the houses they build and eat the fruit of their own vineyards. Unlike the past, invaders will not take their houses and confiscate their vineyards. For my people will live as long as trees, and my chosen ones will have time to enjoy their hard-won gains. They will not work in vain, and their children will not be doomed to misfortune. For they are people blessed by the LORD, and their children, too, will be blessed. I will answer them before they even call to me. While they are still talking about their needs, I will go ahead and answer their prayers! The wolf and the lamb will feed together. The lion will eat hay like a cow. But the snakes will eat dust. In those days no one will be hurt or destroyed on my holy mountain. I, the LORD, have spoken!"

Isaiah 65:17-25 NLT

You often hear people talking about the lion lying down with the lamb but that is actually misquoted from Isaiah 65:25.

"Most importantly, I want to remind you that in the last days scoffers will come, mocking the truth and following their own desires. They will say, 'What happened to the promise that Jesus is coming again? From before the times of our ancestors, everything has remained the same since the world was first created.' They deliberately forget that God made the heavens long ago by the word of his command, and he brought the earth out from the water and surrounded it with water. Then he used the water to destroy the ancient world with a mighty flood. And by the same word, the present heavens and earth have been stored up for fire. They are

Coming Soon: Heaven

being kept for the day of judgment, when ungodly people will be destroyed.

But you must not forget this one thing, dear friends: A day is like a thousand years to the Lord, and a thousand years is like a day. The Lord isn't really being slow about his promise, as some people think. No, he is being patient for your sake. He does not want anyone to be destroyed, but wants everyone to repent. But the day of the Lord will come as unexpectedly as a thief. Then the heavens will pass away with a terrible noise, and the very elements themselves will disappear in fire, and the earth and everything on it will be found to deserve judgment.

Since everything around us is going to be destroyed like this, what holy and godly lives you should live, looking forward to the day of God and hurrying it along. On that day, he will set the heavens on fire, and the elements will melt away in the flames. But we are looking forward to the new heavens and new earth he has promised, a world filled with God's righteousness"

2 Peter 3:3-13 NLT

These two Bible passages, along with Revelation 21 and Isaiah 60, give us very clear descriptions of the New Earth. They tell us some of the characteristics of this new place.

- It is a world filled with God's righteousness.
- It is a place of happiness and a source of joy.
- There will be no more weeping and pain.
- Creation will no longer be carnivorous. Animals won't eat other animals. The wolf and the lamb will feed together and the lion will eat hay.
- God's home will be with people. He will live with them.
- God will be the light of the city.
- Nothing evil is permitted in.

The New Heaven and The New Earth

- There will be nations.
- The nations will bring their produce to Jerusalem.

A distinction must be made here between future human beings and future New Creation Christians. People will still be around, at least for the 1000 year Millennium. The difference between people and God's people who are New Creation Christians is clear. In eternity, New Creation Christians will not marry or be given in marriage and they will receive glorified bodies. They will rule and reign with Jesus and are no longer subject to death. If you are not a New Creation Christian, I would set this book down and become one right now by surrendering your life and future to Jesus Christ, the coming King of planet Earth.

The Bible makes it clear that there will be a New Jerusalem, a heavenly city, but that it comes down to planet earth. Some have said it is suspended over the earth and some have said it will be on the earth. As long as both the New Jerusalem and the New Earth are accessible, the details can be left until we need directions. Israel as a nation and Jerusalem as a city will never cease. The only ones allowed access to the Heavenly Jerusalem are those who belong to Jesus Christ and have their names written in the "Lamb's Book of Life." There is no distinction between Jew and Gentile. All who belong to him are welcome there.

> *"Then I saw a new heaven and a new earth, for the old heaven and the old earth had disappeared. And the sea was also gone. And I saw the holy city, the new Jerusalem, coming down from God out of heaven like a bride beautifully dressed for her husband.*
>
> *I heard a loud shout from the throne, saying, 'Look, God's home is now among his people! He will live with them, and they will be his people. God himself will be with them. He will wipe every tear from*

Coming Soon: Heaven

their eyes, and there will be no more death or sorrow or crying or pain. All these things are gone forever.'

And the one sitting on the throne said, 'Look, I am making everything new!' And then he said to me, 'Write this down, for what I tell you is trustworthy and true.' And he also said, 'It is finished! I am the Alpha and the Omega—the Beginning and the End. To all who are thirsty I will give freely from the springs of the water of life. All who are victorious will inherit all these blessings, and I will be their God, and they will be my children.'"

"I saw no temple in the city, for the Lord God Almighty and the Lamb are its temple. And the city has no need of sun or moon, for the glory of God illuminates the city, and the Lamb is its light. The nations will walk in its light, and the kings of the world will enter the city in all their glory. Its gates will never be closed at the end of day because there is no night there. And all the nations will bring their glory and honor into the city. Nothing evil will be allowed to enter, nor anyone who practices shameful idolatry and dishonesty - but only those whose names are written in the Lamb's Book of Life"

Revelation 21:1-7, 22-27 NLT

The Bible seems to suggest that those who belong to Jesus Christ have access to the New Jerusalem and all of planet Earth as well. That is a far cry from gathering in a big room for an eternal sing-along!

There are some things clearly revealed in Scripture about the New Heaven and the New Earth, and some things we can only speculate about. As we speculate about what will be and won't be in eternity, my question is *why not?*

Why wouldn't the pets you love be there? Why wouldn't we have technology? Why wouldn't there be vehicles that drive and fly? Why wouldn't there be good coffee? Everything that is a part

The New Heaven and The New Earth

of ruling and reigning with God and enjoying him will be included.

Abraham followed God and was looking forward to a promised city that God was building.

> *"Abraham was confidently looking forward to a city with eternal foundations, a city designed and built by God"*
> Hebrews 11:10 NLT.

Amazingly, God himself designed and built the city. What are some of the distinctive characteristics of God's city? The building materials are the precious materials of Earth because the value system of Earth is upside down. Gold is highly sought after on Earth but used as pavement in heaven. The high walls are a sign of our security in God. It is approximately 1500 miles cubed. I read that if each person had a cubical space of one third of a mile, 20 billion people could fit there. I didn't confirm the mathematics of this, but the point is that in my Father's house there is plenty of room. There is free entrance and exit from the city. One commentator said the New Jerusalem is a sphere that rests just above the earth like a moon revolving around it. The wall is jasper or blue white diamonds. John was using human language to describe something brand-new.

Paul mentioned the heavenly city in Galatians 4:26 when he called it *"...the Jerusalem which is above"* (NIV). It is also called the Holy City and Mount Zion. Whatever it is named, it will be beautiful and more perfect than Eden.

In the future, you and I will have access to a perfect Earth created by God, free from all of the ills of this present earth. In addition, we will have access to and possibly live in the Heavenly City of Jerusalem. That is better than Star Wars, and beyond all you can ask, think, or imagine. Our imaginations are limited and therefore it is impossible to completely understand the world and future God is describing to us. I believe you will be amazed daily

Coming Soon: Heaven

as you discover and explore the new world(s) God designed and created for your pleasure and his.

Eternity with God will be a place where the pressures and fears of this life dissipate in the light of his presence. I like to think about heaven as being *all-inclusive*. The endless worries and details of life on planet earth no longer exist. All you need has already been thought about and prepared for. Jesus got the place and the provisions ready for you. You will not be an imposition there, it was made for you.

What Is Our Purpose In Eternity?

> *"But God is so rich in mercy, and he loved us so much, that even though we were dead because of our sins, he gave us life when he raised Christ from the dead. (It is only by God's grace that you have been saved!) For he raised us from the dead along with Christ and seated us with him in the heavenly realms because we are united with Christ Jesus. So God can point to us <u>in all future ages</u> as examples of the incredible wealth of his grace and kindness toward us, as shown in all he has done for us who are united with Christ Jesus"*
>
> Ephesians 2:4-7 NLT

It would be remarkable if God said he had plans for us in the future age, but *in all future ages* is a little beyond all I can ask, think, or imagine. That should completely dispel the idea of a boring future! God has already accomplished an incredible work of mercy and he plans to unveil that work through us to human and spiritual beings in the coming ages. Born again New Creation Christians are to be Exhibit A for all to view. We are to be known as *"the objects of his mercy"* (Romans 9:23 NIV)

Coming Soon: Heaven

In order to see effectively into eternity future, we must begin in eternity past. What happened before man was created and God decided to make them part of his future?

It is important to understand that rebellion against God did not start in Eden. It spread to Eden from heaven where Satan, previously known before his fall as Lucifer (which means the light-bearer), was created by God as one of the archangels, along with Michael and Gabriel. He became proud, and rather than worship God, he wanted to be worshipped. He led one third of the angels in a rebellion against God. They were cast out of heaven (Revelation 12:7-9) where Satan slandered God to Adam and Eve like he had slandered him to the angels. Adam and Eve believed the lie about God, that he was somehow untrustworthy and withholding life's best and optimum from them.

They were cast out of Eden but not before God set in motion a plan to forgive man and use his mercy towards them as an eternal testimony of his true nature. God could have destroyed Satan and the angels when they rebelled, but he wanted to be loved because of his wisdom and goodness, not just out of fear. All of creation would have respected and feared God if he had done that, but they wouldn't be drawn to him in love.

The Bible says that Jesus was *"the Lamb slain before the foundation of the world" (Revelation 13:8).* That implies that before he ever said *"let there be light,"* the plan was already in motion for God to send Jesus as a sacrifice for mankind. Paul spoke about this advance plan in his letter to the Ephesian church.

> *"Even before he made the world, God loved us and chose us in Christ to be holy and without fault in his eyes. God decided in advance to adopt us into his own family by bringing us to himself through Jesus Christ. This is what he wanted to do, and it gave him great pleasure"*
>
> Ephesians 1:4-5 NLT

What Is Our Purpose In Eternity?

In chapter 3 of the same book he says,

> *"God's purpose in all this was to use the church to display his wisdom in its rich variety to all the unseen rulers and authorities in the heavenly places. This was his <u>eternal plan</u>, which he carried out through Christ Jesus our Lord."*
>
> Ephesians 3:10-11 NLT

This plan was God's eternal plan. It wasn't done in response to Satan's rebellion or Adam and Eve's rebellion. God set this plan in motion before the world began. His plan is to use the church to display his wisdom to future ages. In coming days, when an angel wants to lead a rebellion or question the character of God, they will simply have to look at the fruit of God's mercy displayed in redeemed mankind. God is very good and very merciful. New Creation Christians get to declare and demonstrate that for eternity.

Paul goes on to say in Ephesians and elsewhere in the New Testament that God hid this plan in a mystery and didn't tell anyone about it until after it had already been accomplished. I like to compare it to a chess game where a player is sacrificed in the short term only to bring about a game winning check mate. The trap was set and Satan fell in. This mystery was hidden from the prophets, who alluded to it in their writings, the disciples, who thought Jesus was going to immediately set up his kingdom in Israel, the angels, who would like to "look into these things," and especially the devil. He would have never cooperated with Jesus' sacrifice if he knew the end result.

> *"We do, however, speak a message of wisdom among the mature, but not the wisdom of this age or of the rulers of this age, who are coming to nothing. No, we speak of God's secret wisdom, a wisdom that has been hidden and that God destined for our glory before time began. <u>None of the rulers of this age understood it, for if they had,</u>*

Coming Soon: Heaven

> *<u>they would not have crucified the Lord of glory</u>. However, as it is written: "No eye has seen, no ear has heard, no mind has conceived what God has prepared for those who love him…"*
>
> 1 Corinthians 2:6-9 NIV

God's eternal purpose for man is bigger than his job or ministry on the earth. It reaches into the coming ages. What that actually will look like in eternity isn't as clear as we would like it to be. We know looking back at his great wisdom for us and desire to include us in his future and family, that the future must be bright.

I read a story about a doctor who was treating a patient in a treatment room while the doctor's dog tried desperately to get in to its master. The doctor commented that the dog didn't know what was in the room but he wanted in because he knew who was in there, his master. That is a great picture of eternity. We don't know everything about what it will be like but we know who will be there.

In our heart of hearts we know that in light of what he has done, and what he is going to do in the future causes great expectation. Even creation itself can hardly wait.

> *"Yet what we suffer now is nothing compared to the glory he will reveal to us later. For all creation is waiting eagerly for that future day when God will reveal who his children really are. Against its will, all creation was subjected to God's curse. But with eager hope, the creation looks forward to the day when it will join God's children in glorious freedom from death and decay. For we know that all creation has been groaning as in the pains of childbirth right up to the present time. And we believers also groan, even though we have the Holy Spirit within us as a foretaste of future glory, for we long for our bodies to be released from sin and suffering. We, too, wait with eager hope for the day when God will give us our full*

What Is Our Purpose In Eternity?

rights as his adopted children, including the new bodies he has promised us"
Romans 8:18-23 NLT

Your life is bigger than planet earth. I have a poster that says, *True Vision Lights the Way Beyond Success to Eternal Purpose.* Your life and purpose on earth is important, but this life isn't the end. God always wanted to remove the barrier and space that existed between the physical and spiritual worlds. Your eternal purpose is to live in the New Jerusalem, ruling, reigning, and enjoying life on the New Earth. It will be better than Hawaii, and more fun than riding snowmobiles or motorcycles!

Coming Soon: Heaven

What Is My Purpose Now?

In light of your fabulous future, what should you be doing now? The Bible is clear about not getting sidetracked into something other than your true calling and purpose. Paul tells us in several places to set our hearts, minds, and affections on things above. Wisdom may best be defined as, *the ability to know and do what is most important.*

Paul told the Philippian church to live like they weren't really from here.

> *"But <u>we are citizens of</u> <u>heaven</u>, where the Lord Jesus Christ lives. And we are eagerly waiting for him to return as our Savior. He will take our weak mortal bodies and change them into glorious bodies like his own, using the same power with which he will bring everything under his control"*
> Philippians 3:20-21 NLT

Even though we are currently living on this planet, he says our citizenship is somewhere else.

In my twenties, I served as an assistant pastor in Glasgow, Scotland. In order to stay there as an American citizen, it was necessary for me to be invited by a church and then register with the local police. There were certain restrictions on me and I was known as a *resident alien*. We are resident aliens on earth. It is important to always recognize that you live here as an alien or foreigner. Your true allegiance is to your home country. For me, it was America; for Christians our home country is heaven. Always remember, you're not from around here! The apostle Peter tells us,

> *"The Lord isn't really being slow about his promise, as some people think. No, he is being patient for your sake. He does not want anyone to be destroyed, but wants everyone to repent. But the day of the Lord will come as unexpectedly as a thief.*
>
> *Then the heavens will pass away with a terrible noise, and the very elements themselves will disappear in fire, and the earth and everything on it will be found to deserve judgment. <u>Since everything around us is going to be destroyed like this, what holy and godly lives you should live, looking forward to the day of God and hurrying it along</u>. On that day, he will set the heavens on fire, and the elements will melt away in the flames. But we are looking forward to the new heavens and new earth he has promised, a world filled with God's righteousness. And so, dear friends, while you are waiting for these things to happen, make every effort to be found living peaceful lives that are pure and blameless in his sight"*
>
> 2 Peter 3:9-14 NLT

His advice is to live holy as you anticipate the change of the ages. He goes on to say we should live lives filled with peace, purity, and blamelessness. C.S. Lewis said, *"Aim at heaven and you will get earth thrown in. Aim at earth and you get neither"* (The Joyful Christian). Live like a citizen of heaven and even your earthly life will benefit.

Paul tells us where to focus, and Peter tells us how to live. Jesus told us to reach people who didn't yet have a relationship

What Is My Purpose Now?

with him. Since you are spiritually ready for heaven as soon as you make the decision to follow Jesus, your role now is to get others ready for heaven. The more you understand the truth about eternity the more you want to take people with you. A real Biblical revelation of heaven and hell is the best motivator to share this new life with others.

It is very easy to become distracted with life and not be doing what is most important. Remember, wisdom is knowing and doing what matters most. Paul told Timothy to keep his focus by thinking about life as a soldier.

> *"Endure suffering along with me, as a good soldier of Christ Jesus. Soldiers don't get tied up in the affairs of civilian life, for then they cannot please the officer who enlisted them"*
>
> 2 Timothy 2:3-4 NLT

In the same way a soldier doesn't go to a foreign country to fight and then start a farm or get a job, stay focused on your calling.

You shine like a star in the universe as you hold out the word of light and life. You have a specific calling to reach your individual world with the good news of Jesus. Reinhard Bonnke, the German evangelist, talks about his calling to *plunder hell and populate heaven*. That is really the calling of every Christian. Take some people with you into eternity with God. They will be eternally grateful.

In the Old Testament, an angel had a very important message for the prophet Daniel, and it is helpful to us as well.

> *"Many of those whose bodies lie dead and buried will rise up, some to everlasting life and some to shame and everlasting disgrace. Those who are wise will shine as bright as the sky, and those who lead many to righteousness will shine like the stars forever"*
>
> Daniel 12:2-3 NLT

Coming Soon: Heaven

God's dream for you in this life is to influence as many people as possible to follow Jesus. As you live your life as an example, take advantage of every opportunity to share the good news about Jesus Christ that changes lives.

Penn Jillette, a famous Las Vegas comedian, is an atheist. A Christian talked to him about following Jesus and afterwards Penn made this statement, even though he didn't become a Christian,

> *"I've always said that I don't respect people who don't proselytize. I don't respect that at all. If you believe that there's a heaven and a hell, and people could be going to hell or not getting eternal life, and you think that it's not really worth telling them this because it would make it socially awkward—and atheists who think people shouldn't proselytize and who say just leave me alone and keep your religion to yourself—how much do you have to hate somebody to not proselytize?* <u>*How much do you have to hate somebody to believe everlasting life is possible and not tell them that?*</u>
>
> *"I mean, if I believed, beyond the shadow of a doubt, that a truck was coming at you, and you didn't believe that truck was bearing down on you, there is a certain point where I tackle you. And this is more important than that."*

How much do you have to hate somebody to believe everlasting life is possible, and not tell them? Do you believe eternity with Jesus is possible? What are you waiting for?

Heaven Is Eagerly Anticipating Your Arrival!

As pastor of a local church for over thirty-five years, I have had to conduct many funerals. Some of the people I knew better than others. I have friends and family that have gone on into eternity before me. Sometimes just driving down the road or walking in a store, I will be overcome for a moment with grief. We all deal with death differently, but the Holy Spirit is the comforter.

The internet recently told of a Mississippi man, James Breland, who lost his wife, Bilie, to death after over sixty years of marriage. He found the following note written to him from her in his checkbook after she died, *"Please don't cry because I died! Smile because I lived! Know that I'm in a happy place! Know that we will meet again! I'll see you there!"* She was right.

Approximately a year ago, I was driving from one church campus to another, not really thinking about anything in particular. Suddenly, I had a very strong impression, almost a voice in my heart that said, *Heaven loves you*. I was startled and in my mind began to question the Biblical accuracy of what I had just heard.

Coming Soon: Heaven

I knew God loved me, but the impression I received was that there was more than one who loved me in heaven. My mother-in-law had died about a year before that and I specifically thought of her and also a friend from the church who was very dear to me, and often prayed for me. It was a revelation to know I am loved there. It made me aware that there are those in heaven who want me there. When someone dies we say they are going, but heaven says they are coming.

In the Old Testament, there is a strong sense that those who die are going towards something, rather than leaving something. When Jacob was dying he said this,

> "...I am about to be <u>gathered to my people</u>. Bury me with my fathers in the cave in the field of Ephron the Hittite..."
> Genesis 49:29 NIV

Notice the emphasis was on where he was going rather than on where he was leaving.

Paul spoke of the family of God which is represented in two places, heaven and earth.

> "For this reason I bow my knees to the Father of our Lord Jesus Christ, from whom <u>the whole family in heaven and earth</u> is named..."
> Ephesians 3:14-15 NKJV

When a Christian dies, they don't cease to be part of the family. They just move locations, waiting for the time when the entire family is gathered to a huge reunion at the wedding supper of the Lamb. All of your family and friends who followed Jesus will be there along with Paul, Joseph, Daniel, and most of all, Jesus.

Heaven Is Eagerly Anticipating Your Arrival

Heaven is eagerly anticipating your arrival. You are welcome and wanted there. There is a crowd in heaven observing the scene on earth and cheering when another person follows Jesus.

"Therefore, since we are surrounded by such a huge crowd of witnesses to the life of faith, let us strip off every weight that slows us down, especially the sin that so easily trips us up. And let us run with endurance the race God has set before us. [2] We do this by keeping our eyes on Jesus, the champion who initiates and perfects our faith. Because of the joy awaiting him, he endured the cross, disregarding its shame. Now he is seated in the place of honor beside God's throne"

Hebrews 12:1-2 NLT

We are being watched and cheered on. Most of the accounts I have read about those who have died and gone to heaven tell of being greeted by those they knew on earth such as family and friends or even strangers, who were all happy to see them. They couldn't wait to show them around. Your arrival in heaven is eagerly anticipated. Welcome home.

Why Not?

Oftentimes, people focus on the limitations of heaven, but I say let's focus on the possibilities. When someone asks me if something will be in heaven I say, "If it isn't against Scripture, why not?" Randy Alcorn addresses many specific questions about heaven in his book, *Everything you always wanted to know about Heaven*. If this subject piques your interest that would be a good source of further study.

Will we remember in heaven?

Someone said, "Will we be bigger fools in Paradise than we were on the earth?" Of course not. (We are going to a place that is better with more, not a place where we are diminished or in any way less than now.) Throughout the years we have heard that we use less than 10% of our brain. My personal opinion is that sin, the fall in Eden, and the climate changes during the flood of Noah's time have affected the way human's process oxygen. When the curse is lifted off of the earth and man's human bodies, our brains can finally breathe and function at full capacity. That is my opinion. I could use a good shot of oxygen in my brain! The earth hasn't worked right since the curse came on it in Eden. I can't wait until my brain works like God always intended! We will know more and always be learning. Our education about God and his universe will never end. We will not forget what we knew, we will know more in eternity.

Will we still know each other in heaven?

In the story of the rich man and Lazarus it is significant that the rich man recognized Lazarus and had his memory (Luke 16). There is an account in the gospels where Moses and Elijah are with Jesus on the Mount of Transfiguration. The disciples recognized them. They didn't become faceless robots. They kept their identity and uniqueness. Relationships are part of who we are as Christians. Relationships are of God, now and eternally.

> *"After six days Jesus took Peter, James and John with him and led them up a high mountain, where they were all alone. There he was transfigured before them. His clothes became dazzling white, whiter than anyone in the world could bleach them. And there appeared before them Elijah and Moses, who were talking with Jesus. Peter said to Jesus, 'Rabbi, it is good for us to be here. Let us put up three shelters—one for you, one for Moses and one for Elijah.' (He did not know what to say, they were so frightened.)"*
>
> Mark 9:2-6 NIV

Will our pets be there?

Why not? If animals will be there, why not the ones we knew and loved from planet earth? If your pet brought you joy, why would you not enjoy it in heaven? Of course, we know cats will not make it. (Joking…I really like cats)

Will there be vehicles in heaven?

Why wouldn't I have access to a Maserati that can also fly? Technology and knowledge will increase. It wouldn't make any sense for man to revert back to a hunting and gathering society,

Why Not?

now that we know more about science and how the world works. Science simply means "knowledge" and all knowledge is from God. He is all-knowing. Heaven has been unattractive to many because it seemed primitive. The secret sauce is out of the bottle. God has no plans for us to go backward, but only forward. How fast will my Maserati go on the New Earth?

Will there be extinct animals?

Again, why not? If they lived on the earth before they became extinct, why wouldn't they be there in eternity? The good news is that even the Tyrannosaurus Rex would not eat meat (me). God is creative and filled with wonder and joy. I expect great surprises in heaven.

How old will we be in heaven?

Thomas Aquinas believed we would be the same age as Jesus when he died in his early thirties. The Bible doesn't say that, but the idea is that you will be at your peak when you are fully grown, but not losing any physical capacity. That seems to be early thirties. The physical body grows and develops to a certain peak and then things go the other way! It makes sense to be at that peak. Why not?

Will we have privacy or will we always be with the group?

For some of us, it would be difficult for it to be heaven if we always had to be with a crowd. While we will enjoy each other's company, there is a uniqueness and individual relationship between you and God. Jesus spoke of a new name for us, written on a white stone, known only to us and him. In ancient Rome, this stone he spoke about was known as a *tessera*. (It was a small object made of wood, stone, clay or bone, and it conveyed special privileges to its owner. The ancient Romans used tesserae as tokens of admittance to events in the Roman arena.)

> *"....To the one who is victorious, I will give some of the hidden manna. I will also give that person a white stone with a new name written on it, known only to the one who receives it"*
> Revelation 2:17 NIV

The whole idea to me is that you will never lose your uniqueness and individuality.

Will there be travel to other planets?

The answer to this is obvious. This universe belongs to God. He created it and can do anything he wants to it, with it, and in it. There is no reason to believe he has restricted his activity, or will restrict his followers' activities to one area. Interestingly, scientists recently discovered an earth-like planet with very few differences from earth. The only problem is that it is a long way off and unreachable to mankind right now. Why not visit the entire creation? Why did God create the entire universe? Why would he not have a plan for all he has made?

Paul made it clear that there is not and will never be a realm where Jesus Christ is not Lord.

> *"Therefore God exalted him to the highest place and gave him the name that is above every name, that at the name of Jesus every knee should bow, in heaven and on earth and under the earth…"*
> Philippians 2:9-10 NIV

Anywhere there is a place; Jesus will be Lord and master of that place.

Why Not?

There may be many more questions you would like answers to. The point is that heaven should be thought of as a place of unlimited possibilities because of the nature of our unlimited God.

What Others Have Said About Eternity

S ome were right, and some were wrong.

John Lennon sang in his 1971 anthem, *Imagine*

> *Imagine there's no heaven,*
>
> *It's easy if you try,*
>
> *No hell below us,*
>
> *Above us only sky,*
>
> *Imagine all the people living for today...*

Stephen Hawking, *the world-renowned theoretical physicist - finds no room for heaven in his vision of the cosmos. In an interview published in the Guardian newspaper, the 69-year-old says the human brain is like a computer that will stop working when its components fail. 'There is no heaven or afterlife for broken-down computers; that is a fairy story for people afraid of the dark,' Hawking told the paper"* (From Fox News 5/16/2011).

Coming Soon: Heaven

A.W. Tozer *"We must meet the uncertainties of this world with the certainty of the world to come."*

Augustine *"They, then, who are destined to die, need not be careful to inquire what death they are to die, but into what place death will usher them."*

C.S. Lewis *"Though we cannot experience our life as an endless present, we are eternal in God's eyes; that is, in our deepest reality."*

"If you read history you will find that the Christians who did most for the present world were precisely those who thought most of the next."

"When the author walks on the stage the play is over. God is going to invade, all right - something so beautiful to some of us and so terrible to others that none of us will have any choice left? For this time it will be God without disguise. It will be too late then to choose your side."

"Christianity asserts that every individual human being is going to live forever, and this must be either true or false. Now there are a good many things which would not be worth bothering about if I were going to live only seventy years, but which I had better bother about very seriously if I am going to live forever."

"And as He spoke, He no longer looked to them like a lion; but the things that began to happen after that were so great and beautiful that I cannot write them. And for us this is the end of all the stories, and we can most truly say that they all lived happily ever after. But for them it was only the beginning of the real story. All their life in this world and all their adventures in Narnia had only been the cover and the title page: now at last they were beginning Chapter One of the Great Story which no one on earth has read: which goes on forever: in which every chapter is better than the one before." (Written at the end of the Narnia series.)

"Whatever is not eternal is eternally out of date."

What Others Have Said About Eternity

"If I find in myself a desire which no experience in this world can satisfy, the most probable explanation is that I was made for another world."

"I have come home at last! This is the land I have been looking for all my life, though I never knew it till now. The reason why we love old Narnia is that it sometimes looked a little like this."

Fyodor Dostoevsky *"If you were to destroy the belief in immortality in mankind, not only love but every living force on which the continuation of all life in the world depended, would dry up at once."*

Art Lindsley (Ph.D. Senior Fellow, C.S. Lewis Institute) - *"According to the atheist, life comes spontaneously out of the cosmic slime. All life springs from inert or nonliving matter. Life comes from non-life through evolution. Our origin, in other words, is out of death. Since there is no life after death, our destiny is death. What then is the point or value of life? Life is merely an unnecessary chance interruption in the midst of cosmic death. For the believer, on the other hand, God is our creator. We are given the gift of life. Our destiny in Christ is eternal life. Death is merely a very temporary interruption in the midst of cosmic life. Notice the radical contrasts between these views of life. No wonder that atheist Bertrand Russell said that his view led to "unyielding despair." No wonder atheist Albert Camus maintained that, in light of the meaninglessness of this picture of life, the only really serious philosophical question is whether or not to commit suicide."*

Jackson Browne *"I don't know what happens when people die. Can't seem to grasp it as hard as I try. It's like a song I can hear playing right in my ear that I can't sing. I can't help listening."* (From "For a Dancer" written by Jackson Browne. Copyright: Swallow Turn Music)

Helen Keller *"I believe in the immortality of the soul because I have within me immortal longings."*

Thomas Watson *"Eternity to the godly is a day that has no sunset; eternity to the wicked is a night that has no sunrise."*

Coming Soon: Heaven

William *Law* *"If you have not chosen the Kingdom of God first, it will in the end make no difference what you have chosen instead."*

Isaac Watts *"I believe the promises of God enough to venture an eternity on them."*

Alexander MacLaren *"I know what Eternity is, though I cannot define the word to satisfy a metaphysician. The little child taught by some grandmother Lois, in a cottage, knows what she means when she tells him "you will live forever," though both scholar and teacher would be puzzled to put it into other words."*

Randy Alcorn *"After being forcibly evicted from heaven (Isaiah 14:12-15), the devil is bitter not only toward God, but toward us and the place that's no longer his. (It must be maddening for Satan to realize we're now entitled to the home he was kicked out of.) What better way for demons to attack than to whisper lies about the very place God tells us to set our hearts and minds on (Colossians 3:1-2)?"*

David *"David pleaded with God for the child. He fasted and spent the nights lying in sackcloth on the ground. The elders of his household stood beside him to get him up from the ground, but he refused, and he would not eat any food with them. On the seventh day the child died. David's attendants were afraid to tell him that the child was dead, for they thought, While the child was still living, he wouldn't listen to us when we spoke to him. How can we now tell him the child is dead? He may do something desperate. David noticed that his attendants were whispering among themselves, and he realized the child was dead. 'Is the child dead?' he asked. 'Yes,' they replied, 'he is dead.' Then David got up from the ground. After he had washed, put on lotions and changed his clothes, he went into the house of the LORD and worshiped. Then he went to his own house, and at his request they served him food, and he ate. His attendants asked him, 'Why are you acting this way? While the child was alive, you fasted and wept, but now that the child is dead, you get up and eat!'*

What Others Have Said About Eternity

He answered, 'While the child was still alive, I fasted and wept. I thought, Who knows? The LORD may be gracious to me and let the child live. But now that he is dead, why should I go on fasting? Can I bring him back again? I will go to him, but he will not return to me'" 2 Samuel 12:16-22 NIV

Lecrae *"If I'm wrong about God then I wasted my life. If you're wrong about God then you wasted your eternity."*

Jesus *"Let not your heart be troubled; you believe in God, believe also in Me. In My Father's house are many mansions; if it were not so, I would have told you. I go to prepare a place for you. And if I go and prepare a place for you, I will come again and receive you to Myself; that where I am, there you may be also. And where I go you know, and the way you know."*
Thomas said to Him, 'Lord, we do not know where You are going, and how can we know the way?'
Jesus said to him, 'I am the way, the truth, and the life. No one comes to the Father except through Me'" (John 14:1-6 NKJV).

"Jesus said to her, 'I am the resurrection and the life. The one who believes in me will live, even though they die; and whoever lives by believing in me will never die. Do you believe this?'" John 11:25-26 NIV

A Place For You

> "Let not your heart be troubled; you believe in God, believe also in Me. In My Father's house are many mansions; if it were not so, I would have told you. I go to prepare <u>a place for you</u>. And if I go and prepare a place for you, I will come again and receive you to Myself; that where I am, there you may be also"
>
> John 14:1-3 NKJV

Someone said this is the greatest promise ever made, by the greatest person who ever lived, about the greatest place ever imagined. Jesus made his promise of eternity with him very specific and very personal. You will never feel out of place in heaven because it was made just for you. It is your place.

C.S. Lewis said,

> "There have been times when I think we do not desire heaven, but more often I find myself wondering whether, in our heart of hearts, we have ever desired anything else....your place in heaven will seem to be made for you and you alone, because you were made for it stitch by stitch as a glove is made for a hand."

Coming Soon: Heaven

When we think about our home in eternity with God, we often become enamored with the scenery and what it will look like. The views, the smells, and the physicality of a world without a curse will be overwhelming to our senses, I am sure. But the real selling point for heaven is the inner sense that you are finally home. You are finally in the place you were created for, by the one who created you, where you will live forever with those you love. You are much loved and the impact of knowing that on the inside is what heaven really is. The joy and peace on the inside overshadows the scene on the outside.

> *"Then I saw 'a new heaven and a new earth,' for the first heaven and the first earth had passed away, and there was no longer any sea. I saw the Holy City, the new Jerusalem, coming down out of heaven from God, prepared as a bride beautifully dressed for her husband. And I heard a loud voice from the throne saying, 'Look! God's dwelling place is now among the people, and he will dwell with them. They will be his people, and God himself will be with them and be their God. 'He will wipe every tear from their eyes. There will be no more death or mourning or crying or pain, for the old order of things has passed away.' He who was seated on the throne said, 'I am making everything new!' Then he said, 'Write this down, for these words are trustworthy and true.' He said to me: 'It is done. I am the Alpha and the Omega, the Beginning and the End. To the thirsty I will give water without cost from the spring of the water of life. Those who are victorious will inherit all this, and I will be their God and they will be my children'"*
>
> Revelation 21:1-7 NIV

Have you sent in your RSVP yet? Are you coming? I have to say, it would be very hard to understand your decision in light of what we have just discovered if you now rejected heaven. God will support your choice if you choose against it, but he wants you there. So do I.

A Place For You

Pray this prayer from your heart:

> *Jesus, I believe you lived and died for me. You went to the cross where you paid for my sins and spent three days in the heart of the earth. You were raised from the dead and therefore my sins are judged. I receive your forgiveness. I turn from my best religious efforts to save myself and from the things I have done selfishly and in rebellion against you. Forgive me. Save my life and please let me spend eternity in the place you have prepared for me. Amen.*

For Further Study

Everything You Always Wanted to Know About Heaven, Randy C. Alcorn–Tyndale House Publishers–2008.

Heaven, Randy C. Alcorn - Tyndale House Publishers–2004.

In Light of Eternity: Perspectives on Heaven, Randy C. Alcorn-WaterBrook Press – 1999.

The Inspirational writings of C.S. Lewis, C.S. Lewis-Inspirational Press–1994. (This book includes 4 volumes including *The Business of Heaven*)

Heaven is My Home, Paul Scanlon–audio series-PaulScanlon.com

Made in the USA
Columbia, SC
08 November 2024